# Material Matters
# Nonmetals

Carol Baldwin

Chicago, Illinois

Printed and bound in China
08 07 06 05 04
10 9 8 7 6 5 4 3 2

**Library of Congress Cataloging-in-Publication Data:**
Baldwin, Carol, 1943-
  Nonmetals / Carol Baldwin.
    p. cm. -- (Material matters)
Includes bibliographical references and index.
Contents: Properties of nonmetals -- Elements and the periodic table --
Hydrogen -- Carbon -- Nitrogen -- Oxygen -- Phosphorus and sulfur --
Halogens -- Noble gases.
  ISBN 1-4109-0552-7 (lib. bdg.), 1-4109-0939-5 (Pbk.)
  1. Nonmetals--Juvenile literature. [1. Nonmetals. 2. Chemical
elements.] I. Title. II. Series: Baldwin, Carol, 1943-    Material
matters.
  QD161.O93 2004
  546'.7--dc21
                              2003008292

**Acknowledgements**
The Publisher would like to thank the following for permission to reproduce photographs:
Pp. 4–5 N. Wheeler/Robert Harding; pp. 5 (bottom), 19 Science Photo Library; pp. 5 (middle), 14, 17, 31, 32, 35, 39 Getty/Photodisc; pp. 5 (top) 18 (right) Kennedy Space Center/NASA; pp. 6, 34 (right), 38 (left) A. Lambert/Art Directors & Trip; p. 7 (left) Claude Nuridsany & Marie Perennou/Science Photo Library; p. 7 (right) Greg Johnston/Robert Harding; pp. 8, 27 Art Directors & Trip; pp.8–9, 11, 33 (right) Corbis; p. 10 B. Davis/Aspect Picture Library; pp. 10–11 Hutchison Library; pp. 12, 16, 34 (left), 41 Trevor Clifford; p. 13 Andrew Syred/Science Photo Library; p. 14–15 NASA/SOHO; p. 15 Illustrated London News; p. 16–17 Bettmann/Corbis; p. 18 (left) W. Jacobs/Art Directors & Trip; p. 20 Volker Stefer/Science Photo Library; pp. 20–21, 44–45 D. Boone/Corbis; p. 22 (bottom) Peter Menzel/Science Photo Library; p. 22 (top) Dr. Tim Evans/Science Photo Library; p. 23 Phototake/Robert Harding Picture Library; p. 24 Femina/Camera Press; pp. 24–25 Celtic Picture Library/FLPA; pp. 25, 28 Tudor Photography; p. 26 Adam Hart-Davis/Science Photo Library; pp. 26–27 Digital Vision; pp. 28–29 Alwyn/Roberts/FLPA; p. 9 David Taylor Science Photo Library; p. 30 Eye of Science/Science Photo Library; pp. 30—31 ImageState; p. 33 (left) NASA; p. 36 Beanstalk Images/Art Directors & Trip; pp. 36–37 F. Wartenberg/Corbis; p. 37 Hulton Archive; p. 38 (right) S. Adey/Corbis; p. 40 R. White/Corbis; pp. 40–41 George Post/Science Photo Library; p. 42 R. Ressmeyer/Corbis; pp. 42–43 David Brooks/Corbis; p. 43 National Cancer Institute/Science Photo Library.Cover photograph of crystals of quarts (a silicon compound) used with permission of Lawrence Lawry/Science Photo Library.
Every effort has been made to contact copyright holders of any material reproduced in this book. Any omissions will be rectified in subsequent printings if notice is given to the publishers.

# Contents

Some words are shown in bold, **like this.** You can find out what they mean by looking in the glossary. You can also look out for them in the Word Bank at the bottom of each page.

# Nonmetals Everywhere

## Gases in air

The air is made of pure nonmetals and nonmetals that have combined with each other. The **composition** of air is:

- 78% nitrogen
- 21% oxygen
- 0.9% argon
- 0.1% carbon dioxide, neon, helium, krypton, water vapor, and other gases.

As people hike in the hills, the air is clear, cool, and crisp. When they take a deep breath of air, their lungs fill with a **mixture** of nonmetals. Then they look down at the city in the valley far below. Why does the air down there look brownish instead of clear and colorless? More nonmetals are to blame. So what exactly makes up air?

## Gases

Air is a mixture of gases. All the gases in air belong to a group called nonmetals. But not all nonmetals are gases. A few are solids and one is a liquid at room temperature.

- nitrogen
- oxygen
- argon
- carbon dioxide, neon, helium, krypton, water vapor and other gases

This chart shows the proportion of different nonmetals in air.

Many nonmetals are present in the air we breathe. In cities like Los Angeles, they can form **smog**.

Turn to page 26 to find out which nonmetals cause the brownish haze seen over some cities.

**Word Bank**   composition   materials that make up a substance

## Nonmetals in us

The human body is mostly made of nonmetals. About 65 percent of a person's body weight is made of the nonmetal oxygen. Carbon, another nonmetal, makes up 18 percent of the body. Hydrogen makes up 10 percent and nitrogen makes up 3 percent. Metals such as calcium and nonmetals such as phosphorus, sulfur, chlorine, and iodine make up the other 4 percent.

### Fast Fact

Other animals' bodies have different amounts of nonmetals in them. For example, some jellyfish are 95 percent hydrogen and oxygen, in the form of water.

## Find out later . . .

What nonmetal is used as rocket fuel?

What nonmetal is made by plants?

How can you be sure there are no dangerous nonmetals in your home?

mixture   materials combined physically but not chemically
smog   fog-like haze formed by smoke and other air pollutants

5

# Properties of Nonmetals

## Discovering chlorine

In 1774 the Swedish chemist Carl Wilhelm Scheele put a few drops of hydrochloric acid on a piece of manganese dioxide. Within seconds a greenish-yellow gas was given off. He had no idea at the time, but he had just discovered the nonmetal chlorine.

Nonmetals can be solids, liquids, or gases. Most are gases at room temperature. The nonmetal gases are:

- hydrogen
- helium
- nitrogen
- oxygen
- fluorine
- chlorine
- neon
- argon
- krypton
- xenon
- radon

The following nonmetals are solids at room temperature:

- carbon
- phosphorus
- sulfur
- iodine
- astatine

Bromine is the only nonmetal that is a liquid at room temperature.

## Some nonmetals are opaque

Most solids are **opaque**. That means we cannot see light through them. They completely block the light and cause shadows. All metals are opaque. Most nonmetals that are solids are opaque, too. We cannot see light passing through a piece of sulfur. Light does not pass through the **graphite** in pencils, either.

Chlorine is a gas at room temperature.

### Fast Fact
Table salt that we put on our food is a **compound** of the metal sodium and the nonmetal chlorine.

Turn to page 37 to find out about the uses of chlorine.

**Word Bank**     graphite    a form of carbon, used in pencils, lubricants and other products
opaque    not letting light pass through

## Some nonmetals are transparent or translucent

Many liquids are **translucent.** They stop some but not all light from passing through them. Diamond is a solid translucent nonmetal. **Transparent** substances let light pass right through them. A liquid is translucent or transparent depending on its thickness. Light can pass through a thin layer of water. But it cannot pass through a thick layer of water. That is why the deepest parts of the ocean are pitch black. Bromine is similar. Light can pass through a bottle of bromine, but not through a large tank of bromine. Gases are usually transparent. We can see through clean air because it is made of transparent gases.

Turn to page 40 to learn how divers avoid the bends.

The iodine in this dish is a greyish-purple solid. It gives off violet iodine vapor as it is heated.

### Dangerous nitrogen

People breathe in nitrogen in air without a problem. However, nitrogen can cause problems for scuba divers who dive too deep for too long. Nitrogen bubbles form in the body if the diver surfaces too quickly. These bubbles can cause pain, dizziness, loss of feeling, or even death. This is called "the bends."

---

**translucent**   stopping some, but not all, light from passing through
**transparent**   letting light pass through

## Densities of some nonmetals

Metals have very high densities compared to nonmetals. The density of iron is 7.87 grams per cubic centimeter. The metal osmium is three times as dense as this. Even a light metal like aluminum has a density of 2.7 grams per cubic centimeter. Compare this to the densities of some nonmetals in the table below.

## Nonmetals have low densities

Density is a measure of how much **mass** is contained in a certain **volume** of matter, or how many particles of matter are packed into a certain amount of something. You can find the density of something by dividing its mass by its volume. Mass is measured in grams or kilograms. Volume is measured in cubic centimeters or cubic meters. For example, 2 cubic centimeters of lead has a mass of 22.8 grams. So dividing 22.8 grams (mass) by 2 cubic centimeters (volume) gives you a density of 11.4 grams per cubic centimeter.

Nonmetals have lower densities than metals. Carbon's low density is one reason why carbon fibers are used in lightweight fishing rods. The nonmetal gases have very low densities. Helium has a lower density than oxygen and nitrogen in air. Helium-filled balloons will float upward in the air.

The low density of helium is the reason it is used to fill the bodies of blimps.

| Nonmetal | Density (grams per cubic centimeter) |
|---|---|
| Hydrogen | 0.00009 |
| Helium | 0.000179 |
| Oxygen | 0.000143 |
| Nitrogen | 0.000125 |
| Argon | 0.00178 |
| Radon | 0.00973 |
| Chlorine | 0.00321 |
| Phosphorus | 1.82 |
| Sulfur | 2.07 |
| Carbon | 2.27 |
| Bromine | 3.2 |

**Word Bank**   atoms   smallest particle of an element
compound   substance made of different kinds of atom joined together

## Forming compounds

Nonmetals can join with other nonmetals or metals to form **compounds**. For example, water is a compound of two nonmetals. Hydrogen and oxygen join to form water. Carbon dioxide gas in air is another compound. It is made of carbon and oxygen that have joined together. Sugar is a compound made of carbon, hydrogen, and oxygen.

Nonmetals also join with metals like copper, sodium, and iron. Common table salt is a compound of sodium and chlorine. Rust on an old car is a compound of iron and oxygen. Copper, sulfur, and oxygen form the green compound that coats the Statue of Liberty.

### Diatomic gases

Like all materials, nonmetals are made of tiny particles called **atoms**. Some nonmetal atoms join in pairs. They form what we call **diatomic** gases. Diatomic means "two atoms." Hydrogen, nitrogen, chlorine, and fluorine are also diatomic gases.

In this diagram, the black bar represents the strong bond between the two hydrogen atoms.

>>>>>>>
Turn to page 12 to learn more about atoms.

An air-filled object can float on water because the air inside is less dense than water.

**density**   mass of a certain volume of something
**diatomic**   atoms of an element joined in pairs

## Nonmetals are brittle

Metals are **malleable.** That means they can be easily bent or formed into a new shape. Metals are also **ductile.** That means they can be stretched to form wires. Nonmetals are neither malleable nor ductile. All solid nonmetals are **brittle.** That means they will break rather than bend or stretch. **Graphite,** the form of carbon used in pencils, is brittle. We know that it is brittle because pencil points often break. Diamond, the form of carbon used in jewelry, will shatter when it is hit very hard.

## Nonmetals are not shiny

Solid nonmetals do not have a metallic **luster** either. That means they do not shine like the polished surface of a metal such as gold. Solid nonmetals usually look dull, like graphite.

Malleable metals like silver can be hammered or shaped without breaking.

**Word Bank**

brittle    firm, but easily broken
conductor    material that heat or electricity can easily pass through

## Nonmetals are poor conductors

Unlike metals, nonmetals are not good **conductors** of heat. That means heat does not travel quickly or easily through them. Things that are poor conductors of heat are usually said to be good **insulators.** Air is a good insulator. Birds fluff up their feathers in cold weather. This traps air between their feathers and helps keep them warm. People also wear down jackets because air trapped between the down feathers is a good insulator.

Nonmetals, except for graphite, are also good insulators and poor conductors of electricity. In winter, dry indoor air is a good insulator. If you walk across a carpet, your body builds up an electric charge because the static electricity created as you walk cannot escape through the nonmetal air or carpet. Only when you touch something metal, like a doorknob, can the electrical charge flow off your body. You might feel a small electric shock as this happens.

### Phosphorus versus copper

Unlike the nonmetal phosphorus, the metal copper is a good conductor of electricity. Unlike phosphorus, copper is also a good conductor of heat. Because of this, many cooking pans are made with copper.

Electrical wiring in buildings is usually made of copper wire. It is both a good conductor and fairly cheap.

Like other solid nonmetals, sulfur is brittle.

ductile    able to be drawn into a wire
insulator    material that is difficult for heat or electricity to pass through

11

# The Periodic Table

The heads of these matches contain the nonmetal phosphorus. The chemical symbol for phosphorus is P.

## Atoms and ions

Matter can be broken down into very tiny pieces called **atoms.** Most of the **mass** of an atom is in its **nucleus.** This center part of the atom is made of two kinds of particles. **Protons** are particles with a tiny positive electrical charge. **Neutrons** are particles that are neutral, or have no charge.

**Electrons** are particles with a tiny negative electrical charge. In an atom, the number of electrons is the same as the number of protons. Their electrical charges balance. So the atom is neutral. Sometimes, however, atoms can gain or lose one or more electrons. Then they become **ions.** Ions have either extra positive or extra negative electrical charges.

## Symbols of elements

Chemical symbols are a short way of writing the names of the elements. Symbols are either one or two letters, and the first is always a capital letter. Some symbols are the first letter or first two letters of an element's name. Other elements have two-letter symbols that are not the first two letters of their names.

**Key**

| | |
|---|---|
| ☐ | metals |
| ◻ | metalloids |
| ◻ | nonmetals |

**Example**

group number · name

2
beryllium

**Be** — symbol

| 1 hydrogen **H** | 2 | | | | | | | |
|---|---|---|---|---|---|---|---|---|
| lithium **Li** | beryllium **Be** | | | | | | | |
| sodium **Na** | magnesium **Mg** | | | | | | | |

**The Transition Metals**

| | | 3 | 4 | 5 | 6 | 7 | 8 | 9 |
|---|---|---|---|---|---|---|---|---|
| potassium **K** | calcium **Ca** | scandium **Sc** | titanium **Ti** | vanadium **V** | chromium **Cr** | manganese **Mn** | iron **Fe** | cobalt **Co** |
| rubidium **Rb** | strontium **Sr** | yttrium **Y** | zirconium **Zr** | niobium **Nb** | molybdenum **Mo** | technetium **Tc** | ruthenium **Ru** | rhodium **Rh** |
| cesium **Cs** | barium **Ba** | | hafnium **Hf** | tantalum **Ta** | tungsten **W** | rhenium **Re** | osmium **Os** | iridium **Ir** |
| francium **Fr** | radium **Ra** | | rutherfordium **Rf** | dubnium **Db** | seaborgium **Sg** | bohrium **Bh** | hassium **Hs** | meitnerium **Mt** |

**Word Bank**  element  substance made of only one kind of atom
ion  atom or group of atoms that has an electric charge

## Elements

Not all atoms have the same number of protons, neutrons, and electrons. Over a hundred different kinds of atoms have been discovered. Each kind of atom is an **element.** An atom is the basic unit of an element. Sometimes different kinds of elements join together to form a **compound.** Sand is a compound of the elements silicon and oxygen.

## Grouping elements

Elements are grouped in a chart called the **periodic table.** The vertical columns are called groups. All elements in a group have similar properties because their electrons are arranged in similar patterns. A thick, stepped line in the table separates the metals from the other elements. Except for hydrogen, all the nonmetals are on the right-hand side of the periodic table.

## Metalloids

Some elements are neither metals nor nonmetals. These elements are called **metalloids.** They have properties of both metals and nonmetals. Silicon and arsenic are examples of metalloids. They are both used in computer chips and solar cells.

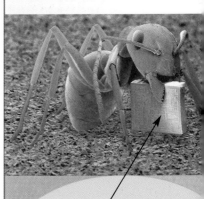

Silicon chips are now so small an ant can carry one. Metalloids are used in computer chips because they conduct electricity in special ways.

|  |  |  |  |  |  | 19 |
|---|---|---|---|---|---|---|
|  |  |  |  |  |  | helium |
|  |  |  |  |  |  | **He** |
| 13 | 14 | 15 | 16 | 18 |  |  |
| boron | carbon | nitrogen | oxygen | fluorine | neon |  |
| **B** | **C** | **N** | **O** | **F** | **Ne** |  |
| aluminum | silicon | phosphorus | sulfur | chlorine | argon |  |
| **Al** | **Si** | **P** | **S** | **Cl** | **Ar** |  |

| 10 | 11 | 12 | 13 | 14 | 15 | 16 | 18 |  |
|---|---|---|---|---|---|---|---|---|
| nickel | copper | zinc | gallium | germanium | arsenic | selenium | bromine | krypton |
| **Ni** | **Cu** | **Zn** | **Ga** | **Ge** | **As** | **Se** | **Br** | **Kr** |
| palladium | silver | cadmium | indium | tin | antimony | tellunum | iodine | xenon |
| **Pd** | **Ag** | **Cd** | **In** | **Sn** | **Sb** | **Te** | **I** | **Xe** |
| platinum | gold | mercury | thallium | lead | bismuth | polonium | astatine | radon |
| **Pt** | **Au** | **Hg** | **Tl** | **Pb** | **Bi** | **Po** | **At** | **Rn** |
| ununnilium | unununium | ununbium |  | ununquadium |  |  |  |  |
| **Uun** | **Uuu** | **Uub** |  | **Uuq** |  |  |  |  |

Turn to page 40 to learn about Group 18, the noble gases.

**metalloids** elements that have properties of both metals and nonmetals
**nucleus** dense, positively charged center of an atom

# Hydrogen

## Hydrogen in the earth's atmosphere

There is very little hydrogen gas in the earth's **atmosphere**. Suppose you had 100 million gallons of air. Of that air, only about 5 gallons would be hydrogen. That is a very small amount when you think about how much of the universe is made of hydrogen.

Hydrogen is the simplest of all the **atoms.** It is made of a single **proton,** circled by a single electron. Hydrogen is the most common **element** in the universe. It is the main element found in all stars. Huge amounts of hydrogen also exist in space between the stars. About 930 out of every 1,000 atoms in the universe are hydrogen atoms. About 69 out of every 1,000 atoms are helium atoms. Atoms of all the other elements make up the remaining 0.1 percent. Because there are too many atoms in the universe to even begin to count, there are still plenty of atoms of all the other elements.

Air contains just 0.000005 percent hydrogen, but 93 percent of atoms in the universe are hydrogen.

At its center, the Sun changes hydrogen to helium at a rate of 700 million tons every second.

**Word Bank**

atmosphere   layer of gases that surrounds the earth
flammable   easily set on fire

## Hydrogen gas

Hydrogen gas is a **diatomic** gas made of two atoms of hydrogen joined together. The symbol for the gas is written as $H_2$ to show that the two atoms are joined. Hydrogen gas has no **odor** or taste and is completely colorless. That means you really cannot tell when it is present. Hydrogen has the lowest density of any gas. People often say this means that hydrogen is lighter than air. A balloon filled with hydrogen will rise and float away when it is released.

Hydrogen is a very **flammable** gas. When hydrogen burns, it joins with oxygen very quickly, releasing huge amounts of heat.

## Hydrogen disaster

Hydrogen's low density gives it great lifting power. The gas was once used in blimps and **zeppelins**. As the large zeppelin *Hindenburg* tried to land in New Jersey in 1937, it burst into flames and crashed.

After the *Hindenburg* accident, hydrogen was no longer used in airships.

## Car batteries

Sometimes a car battery goes "dead" and the car will not start. People often recharge the battery so it will work again but they have to be careful. The battery contains a strong acid. Recharging it produces hydrogen gas. A spark or flame near the battery can make it explode.

## Extracting hydrogen from acids

Acids such as vinegar, hydrochloric acid, and sulfuric acid contain hydrogen. A **chemical reaction** can be used to produce hydrogen gas from an acid. One way to produce hydrogen gas is the reaction between an acid and a metal. In 1766 the English chemist Henry Cavendish produced hydrogen gas by adding some zinc metal to an acid. This method is still used to make small amounts of hydrogen gas in labs. A **mixture** of hydrogen and air in a test tube produces a small explosion when brought near a flame.

### Fast Fact
To test for hydrogen in the lab, a lighted splint is held in the mouth of a test tube of the gas. The burning splint causes a tiny explosion if hydrogen is present.

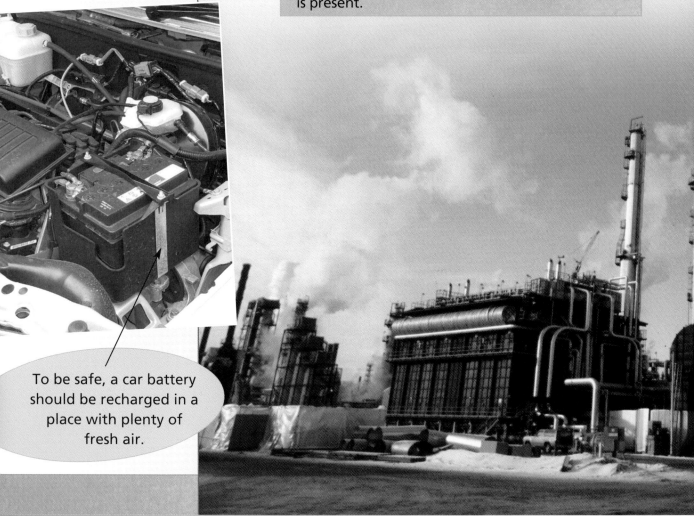

To be safe, a car battery should be recharged in a place with plenty of fresh air.

**Word Bank**     chemical reaction   change that produces one or more new substances
coke   form of carbon made from coal

## Hydrogen and water

On the earth, the most common **compound** of hydrogen is water. When water forms, two atoms of hydrogen join with one **atom** of oxygen. So the chemical formula for water is $H_2O$. Water is used to produce large amounts of hydrogen gas.

Hydrogen is usually made by breaking water apart. Steam is passed over hot carbon in the form of **coke**. The steam reacts with the coke to produce **carbon monoxide** and hydrogen gases. These two gases can easily be separated. Sometimes, however, the two gases are left mixed together. This mixture is used as a **fuel** by industry and is called "water gas." Both hydrogen and water gas are **compressed** and stored in cylinders.

The "water gas reaction" can produce large amounts of hydrogen gas. Hydrogen is used to make fertilizers, rocket fuel, and hydrochloric acid.

### Water maker

The reaction of hydrogen and oxygen to form water gave hydrogen its name. The name comes from the Greek words *hydro*, meaning "water" and *genes*, meaning "forming." The German word for hydrogen is *wasserstoff*, meaning "water stuff."

compressed   squeezed into a smaller space
fuel   any material that can be burned to produce useful heat or power

Hydrogen can be extracted from coal, but this is not good for the environment.

## Hydrogen compounds

Hydrogen joins with carbon and oxygen to form many compounds. These include sugars, starches, fats, and proteins. These compounds are found in all living things. Hydrogen is also found in coal, natural gas, and crude oil products such as gasoline and paraffin.

Large amounts of liquid hydrogen are used in rockets that allow the space shuttle to blast into space.

**Word Bank**    cholesterol   fatty substance in some foods that can clog blood vessels
dissolve   to mix completely and evenly

## Hydrogen is used to make ammonia

Large amounts of hydrogen are used to make ammonia. Ammonia, $NH_3$, is a colorless gas with a strong odor. It is a **compound** of nitrogen and hydrogen. It **dissolves** easily in water and is used in many household cleaning products. Ammonia is also used to make **fertilizers** for growing crops.

## Hydrogen is used to get metals

Many metals that we use are found combined with oxygen. These compounds are called **oxides.** The metals have to be separated from the oxygen before we can use them. One way of doing this is by using hydrogen. For example, hydrogen will react with copper oxide to produce copper and water. The same process can be used to get silver and iron metals.

## Hydrogen is used in foods

Vegetable oils, such as peanut oil and coconut oil, are liquids. Vegetable oil is often treated with hydrogen. During this process the oil changes to a solid, such as margarine. Margarine contains less **cholesterol** than butter. Cholesterol is a fatty substance that can clog blood vessels. So many people use margarine as a substitute for butter.

## Hydrogen is used as rocket fuel

Liquid hydrogen is an important rocket **fuel.** The main engines of the space shuttle use liquid hydrogen and liquid oxygen in two separate tanks. The hydrogen and oxygen are pumped together. Hydrogen burns in oxygen to produce hot steam. The steam rushes out of openings in the bottom of the engines. This pushes the shuttle upward.

### Pure power

Hydrogen is being studied as a fuel for cars, trucks, and buses. When hydrogen and oxygen are combined to make water, electricity can be produced. That is what a hydrogen fuel cell does. The electricity runs the car's motor.

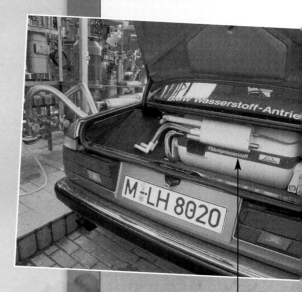

In a car with a hydrogen fuel cell, the only thing that comes from the car's exhaust pipe is water vapor. That means the car does not add **pollution** to the air.

fertilizer   chemicals added to soil to help plants grow better
pollution   contamination by harmful substances in the air, in water, or on land

19

# Carbon

This is a magnified photo of a drill covered in **synthetic** diamonds. These are used by dentists. The diamond fragments are hard enough to cut through teeth.

Carbon is found in different forms and in many different **compounds.** It is in us, in the food you eat, and in the clothes you wear. It is also found in your pencils and in expensive jewelry.

## Diamond

One form of carbon is diamond. In diamond, the carbon **atoms** are packed in a tight, repeating pattern. Each carbon atom is joined to four others. Diamond has a high **density** and is very hard. In fact, diamond is the hardest substance known. But diamond is also very **brittle.** It will shatter if hit with a hammer.

Most diamonds are colorless, but they can be blue, pink, yellow, or other colors. Colored diamonds are rare and often very valuable. The best diamonds are used in jewelry. Other diamonds are used for cutting and grinding.

### Synthetic diamonds

Diamonds can be made from graphite. This is done by heating graphite to very high temperatures under very high pressure. Diamonds made in this way are not thought to be as beautiful as natural diamonds, but they are just as hard and can be used in industry.

After they are mined, diamonds are cut and polished to bring out the beauty of the gems.

**Word Bank**    lubricant   slippery substance used to make machine parts move smoothly and easily

## Graphite

Another form of carbon is graphite. Unlike diamond, graphite has a low density. The carbon atoms in graphite are joined together in layers, like pages in a book. The layers are not held together very strongly. This allows the layers to slide over each other. So graphite feels soft and slippery. Graphite is used as a **lubricant** in places such as the tracks of sliding doors.

## Coal

Coal is a **mixture** of carbon, compounds that contain carbon and hydrogen, and many other impurities. It is an important source of energy for factories and homes. Hard coal contains about 80 percent carbon by **mass.** Soft coal contains about 40 to 50 percent carbon. When coal is heated without air, the other compounds burn off, leaving a form of carbon called coke. Coke is used in making iron and steel.

## Buckyballs

In 1985 a new form of carbon was discovered in England. In the new form, 60 carbon atoms are arranged in a way that makes them look like a soccer ball. These forms of carbon became known as buckyballs. Buckyballs were named after Buckminster Fuller, a man who built domes with interlocking pieces.

This diagram shows how carbon atoms are joined in a buckyball molecule. Scientists are still trying to find ways to use buckyballs.

### Fast Fact

The largest diamond ever found is called the Cullinan diamond. Its mass is 1.3 pounds (0.6 kilograms). That is as much as a dozen eggs.

## DNA

DNA is a chemical found in all our body cells. The small units in the drawing are groups of atoms. They contain carbon, hydrogen, nitrogen, and phosphorus. The order in which the units are lined up is a code. Your cells use the code to make new cells. Every person has a unique DNA code.

## Carbon in living things

Carbon compounds in living things are called **organic compounds**. In animals **proteins** make up cartilage, tendons, and other body tissues. Proteins are long chains of smaller organic compounds. DNA is a code telling our body how to put these compounds together in the right order. For our bodies to make proteins, we must eat and digest proteins from foods. Meat, fish, beans, and dairy products are good sources of protein.

Blood or hair at a crime scene can be tested for DNA. This can help police find the person who committed the crime.

**Carbohydrates** are organic compounds of carbon, hydrogen, and oxygen. Starch and sugar are carbohydrates. Fruits, vegetables, and pasta contain starch and sugar and are good sources of the carbohydrates our bodies need for energy.

Woolly mammoths once roamed the northern parts of Europe, Asia, and North America. Carbon dating revealed that one fossil mammoth from Canada died about 30,000 years ago.

**Word Bank**    carbohydrate    compound that contains carbon, hydrogen, and oxygen
fossil    hardened remains of an ancient plant or animal

Cooking oils, fat in meat, and butter are examples of **lipids.** We need these compounds of carbon, hydrogen, and oxygen to keep our cells working properly. But eating too many foods that contain lipids could be harmful.

Insect remains trapped in amber can be dated using carbon dating. This tells scientists whether the insect might have sucked dinosaur blood!

## Carbon dating

Plants take in carbon in the form of carbon dioxide. They use carbon dioxide to make their own food. Animals take in carbon by eating plants or other animals.

Some carbon **atoms** in living things change over time. This works something like an hourglass where sand grains pour one by one from the top to the bottom. In a similar way, the carbon atoms change one by one into different **elements.**

When a plant or animal dies, the number of these carbon atoms in its body starts to drop. Scientists can measure how much of this carbon is left in its body. So they can figure out how long ago the plant or animal died. This is called **carbon dating** and is one way scientists learn how old **fossils** are.

Turn back to page 19 to find out how lipids such as cholesterol can be harmful.

## The dating game

Many things can be dated using carbon. They include:

- wood, twigs, and seeds
- leather (animal skins)
- coprolites (fossilized animal dung)
- bone
- charcoal
- hair
- eggshells
- antlers and horns
- fish and insect remains
- seashells

**lipid**   organic compound that includes fats and oils
**organic compound**   compound that contains carbon

## The greenhouse effect

Burning fuels like coal helps to increase the **greenhouse effect.** The greenhouse effect is the warming of climates around the world. It is caused by an increase in the amount of carbon dioxide and other gases in the earth's atmosphere.

Carbon dioxide traps heat radiating out from the earth in the same way that glass traps heat in a greenhouse.

## Carbon dioxide

All animals produce carbon dioxide when their cells use food. They give off this gas when they breathe out. Carbon dioxide also forms when carbon burns in air. When wood or other **fuels** burn, carbon in the fuel combines with oxygen in the air. The burning of **fossil fuels,** such as coal, natural gas, and oil products, adds a lot of carbon dioxide to the air. Volcanoes also give off carbon dioxide.

Luckily, plants use carbon dioxide to make their own sugars. This helps to balance the carbon dioxide that is added to the air. However, cutting down forests means that less carbon dioxide is removed from the air. This allows carbon dioxide levels in the air to increase. More carbon dioxide in the air can change the earth's climate.

**Word Bank**   carbon monoxide   poisonous gas produced as carbon burns when there is not enough oxygen

## Carbon monoxide

If carbon burns when there is not enough oxygen, it forms a gas called **carbon monoxide**. Carbon monoxide is a very **poisonous** gas. It keeps blood from carrying enough oxygen to body cells. Even a small amount of carbon monoxide can cause sleepiness and headaches. A gas fire or a car left running in a closed garage can produce enough carbon monoxide to kill someone.

Carbon monoxide detectors help save lives. A loud alarm lets people know if they are in danger. Homes should have carbon monoxide detectors on each floor. At least one should be located near the bedrooms. People who use portable heaters in tents or cabins can use battery-operated detectors.

Burning carbon-containing fuels such as coal to produce electricity adds carbon dioxide to the air.

### Dry ice

When carbon dioxide is frozen at $-108\ °F$ ($-78\ °C$), it is called **dry ice**. It is a lot colder than ice made from water. It can be used to keep foods frozen when they are shipped. As it warms, it changes directly from a solid to a gas.

Dry ice has a big advantage over water ice. There are no messy puddles of liquid when a package of frozen food arrives at its destination.

**dry ice**   frozen carbon dioxide
**fossil fuel**   fuel found in the earth, formed from dead plants and animals.

# Nitrogen

## Air pollution

Nitrogen **oxides** form when nitrogen joins with oxygen. Car exhausts release nitrogen oxides into the air. They add to air pollution in many cities. Nitrogen dioxide can join with water in air to form nitric acid. The acid droplets fall to the earth when it rains. This is called acid rain.

The air around us is made mostly of nitrogen. It makes up 78 percent of the air we breathe. We take in large amounts of nitrogen every time we breathe. But we do not notice it because nitrogen has no color, no **odor,** and no taste.

Nitrogen is a **diatomic** gas, so the symbol for the gas is written as $N_2$ to show that its **atoms** are joined in pairs. Nitrogen gas does not react very easily with other **elements** or **compounds.** Even so, it still forms hundreds of thousands of compounds. These compounds are very important for industries, farming, and living things. Some of these compounds also cause **pollution.**

Acid droplets can damage buildings, statues, and living things.

**Word Bank**    boiling point    temperature at which a liquid changes to a gas

## Producing nitrogen

About 30 million tons of nitrogen gas are produced each year. Almost all of this is produced from air. Air is cooled to a very low temperature where it becomes liquid. Then it is slowly warmed. Each of the gases that make up air has a different **boiling point**. So as the air warms, each gas boils off separately. Nitrogen, which has a boiling point of about −320 °F (−196 °C), is separated from the rest of the air and collected in tanks.

One of the uses of nitrogen gas is in the oil industry. Compressed nitrogen gas is pumped down oil wells. The pressure of the gas forces the oil upward to the surface.

The brownish smog seen over some cities is due to the presence of nitrogen dioxide in the air.

Nitrogen gas rushes into an airbag at up to 200 miles (322 kilometers) per hour.

## Saving the apples

Fruit begins to rot mainly because it reacts with oxygen in the air. But nitrogen gas can be used to keep the picked fruit fresh. Apples can be stored for up to two years if they are kept at low temperatures in sealed rooms filled with nitrogen gas.

Nitrogen cycles through the living and nonliving parts of the world.

# Nitrogen and living things

All living things need many **compounds** that contain nitrogen. Nitrogen occurs in many forms. But most living things cannot use nitrogen gas in air. Nitrogen is changed into useable compounds in two main ways.

- Some **bacteria** in soil and plant roots change nitrogen gas into nitrogen compounds. Plants use the nitrogen compounds to make **proteins.** When animals eat plants, they take in these plant proteins. Then the animals use them to make new proteins.

- When lightning passes through the air, it changes nitrogen gas to nitrogen compounds. These nitrogen compounds combine with rain water and form new compounds that plants can take in and use.

When dead animals and plants **decay,** simple nitrogen compounds form. Bacteria change some of these compounds back into nitrogen gas. The gas returns to the air. This movement of nitrogen is called the **nitrogen cycle.**

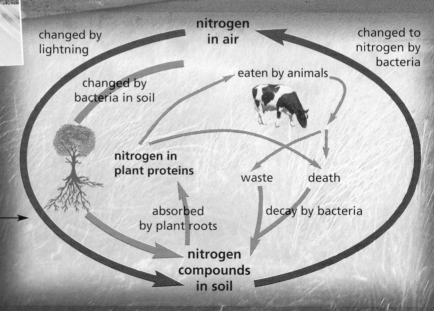

changed by lightning

changed to nitrogen by bacteria

**nitrogen in air**

eaten by animals

changed by bacteria in soil

**nitrogen in plant proteins**

waste

death

absorbed by plant roots

decay by bacteria

**nitrogen compounds in soil**

**Word Bank**   decay   rot
**bacteria**   tiny living things too small to be seen except with a microscope

## Uses of nitrogen

Modern farming often uses up most of the nitrogen compounds found in soil. So **fertilizers** are added to the soil. Many fertilizers are made from ammonia, a compound of nitrogen and hydrogen.

Another important use of nitrogen is in making nitric acid. Nitric acid is a compound of hydrogen, nitrogen, and oxygen. It is used to make fertilizers and explosives such as dynamite. It is also used to make nylon and other plastics.

Other nitrogen compounds are added to some canned and other preserved foods. They help stop the growth of harmful bacteria in the foods. Dentists use nitrous **oxide,** better known as "laughing gas." The sweet-smelling gas helps make patients more relaxed and the treatment less painful.

➤➤➤➤➤➤➤➤➤➤➤➤➤

Turn to pages 30 and 31 to find out how other nonmetals cycle through our world.

### Liquid nitrogen

Nitrogen becomes a liquid at −320 °F (−196 °C). That is very cold. A rubber ball placed in liquid nitrogen for just a few seconds becomes very **brittle.** If you tried to bounce it, it would shatter like glass into tiny pieces.

As liquid nitrogen is poured, its cold temperature condenses water vapor from the air around it.

**nitrogen cycle**   circular pathway in which nitrogen moves through the world

# Oxygen

### Fruit flies

Just a few minutes after being sliced, apples turn brown. This is because oxygen in the air combines with the fruit. Now scientists may have a new way to prevent this. They hope to make a spray from a **protein** found in houseflies that would stop chopped fruit from turning brown.

## Properties and uses of oxygen

Oxygen is a **diatomic** gas with no color, no **odor,** and no taste. It makes up 21 percent of the air. We make most oxygen from air. Air is cooled until it becomes liquid. Then it is slowly warmed. The other main parts of air—nitrogen and argon—boil off first. This leaves oxygen. Most oxygen is used as a compressed gas.

## Importance of oxygen

People need oxygen gas to live. **Fuels** like oil and gas need oxygen to burn. So your home could not be heated without oxygen. Cars and buses could not run. You might think it would be better if there were more oxygen in the air. However, with more oxygen, things would burn more easily and quickly. That could be dangerous.

oxygen        carbon dioxide

A fruit preservative made from a housefly protein would be much cheaper than chemical preservatives.

Plants release oxygen into the air and absorb the carbon dioxide that animals breathe out.

**Word Bank**   photosynthesis   process by which green plants use sunlight, water, and carbon dioxide to make their own food

## Oxygen and living things

Each time you breathe, you take in oxygen and breathe out some carbon dioxide. Plants take in carbon dioxide from the air. They release oxygen into the air.

Living things use much of the oxygen that is given off by plants during **respiration.** In respiration, sugars combine with oxygen. This process releases the energy that living things need. It also produces carbon dioxide and other products. Animals breathe out the carbon dioxide they produce. Plants release some of the carbon dioxide they produce during respiration through their leaves and other plant parts.

### Fast Fact
Without oxygen, a person could live for only about five minutes.

Most of the oxygen in the air comes from plants.

### Food factories
Plants make their own food using a process called **photosynthesis.** They make food from carbon dioxide gas in the air and from water that their roots take from the ground. Plants use energy from sunlight to change the carbon dioxide and water into sugars and oxygen.

**respiration**   process in which a living thing takes in oxygen and uses it to produce energy, giving off carbon dioxide

Oxygen masks drop down and let people breathe if the oxygen level drops in an airplane.

### Fast Facts
- When things burn in air, oxygen is being used up.
- All fires need **fuel**, oxygen, and heat to burn.

## Oxygen compounds

Oxygen combines with almost every **element.** So there are far too many oxygen **compounds** to describe. Water is the most important oxygen compound. It is a compound of oxygen and hydrogen. It is one of the most common compounds on the earth.

Oxygen makes up nearly half of the earth's **crust.** It is found in many rocks and **minerals** in the earth's crust. The most common oxygen compounds in the earth's crust are **oxides.** An oxide is a compound of oxygen and another element. Many oxides, such as iron oxide, are **ores** from which we get important metals.

Oxygen also forms oxides that are gases. These include carbon dioxide and several nitrogen oxides.

## Ozone

Oxygen also exists as a **triatomic** gas called **ozone,** $O_3$. Unlike ordinary oxygen, ozone has a faintly blue color. It also has a strong **odor.** Ozone can be produced by electricity passing through air. People sometimes notice it during storms with lightning. They might also notice it around electrical motors in subway and railroad stations.

ore   metal that is found combined with other elements
ozone   form of oxygen made of three oxygen atoms joined together

There is a layer of ozone in the upper part of the earth's **atmosphere.** This ozone protects the earth's surface from the harmful rays of the Sun. These rays can cause sunburn and skin cancer. Without the ozone layer, most living things on the earth would be killed. In recent years, scientists have become concerned because the ozone layer is being destroyed. Chemicals that people release into the air are causing this problem.

The colors in this satellite photo show where ozone is present in the atmosphere. The dark area over the South Pole shows where ozone has been destroyed.

One way to avoid breathing in ozone is to wear a face mask.

### Bad ozone

Ozone is not always helpful. Ozone is given off by car exhausts. Near the ground, ozone is a **pollutant.** It can harm people's lungs when they breathe it. Older people and children should not exercise outdoors when there is a lot of ozone in the air.

**pollutant**   harmful substance in the air, in water, or on land
**triatomic**   three atoms of the same element joined together

# Phosphorus and Sulfur

## Safety matches

The striking surface on a book of safety matches is made from a **mixture** of red phosphorus and powdered glass. When the head of a match is rubbed across it, some red phosphorus changes to white phosphorus. The white phosphorus bursts into flame and makes the matchstick burn.

Matches used to be made of white phosphorus. Not only was this **toxic**, it easily burst into flame if the matchbox was shaken or left in sunlight.

## Phosphorus

Phosphorus exists in three different forms. White phosphorus is a pale, waxy solid. Red phosphorus is a dark reddish powder. Black phosphorus is a flaky solid that forms when white phosphorus is put under high pressure. Below 95 °F (35 °C), white phosphorus reacts with oxygen in the air and begins to glow. But if the air temperature is above 95 °F, white phosphorus bursts into flames and is converted to red phosphorus. Red phosphorus is much less active.

All living things need phosphorus. It is in all DNA and in our bones and teeth. About 20 percent of the human skeleton is made of calcium phosphate. A phosphate is a **compound** of phosphorus, oxygen, and another **element.** Most phosphorus is found in the form of phosphate rock. Phosphorus from this rock is used in making **fertilizers** for crops. Plants need phosphorus to grow.

**Phosphorus**

Highly Flammable · Toxic

White phosphorus must be stored in water to keep it from reacting with oxygen in the air. Red phosphorus is much more stable.

**Word Bank**   geyser   vent that shoots hot water and steam from underground

# Sulfur

Sulfur is a brittle, yellow solid. It is often found at the edges of volcanoes and around the edges of some hot springs and **geysers.** Sulfur burns with a blue flame. Underground deposits of sulfur are found in Texas and Louisiana, and also in Mexico and Poland.

Sulfur and its compounds are used in fireworks, explosives, paints, plastics, and dyes. Sulfur dioxide is used to keep some foods from rotting. It is also used as a bleach for cloth and for **wood pulp** used in making paper.

Most sulfur is used to make sulfuric acid. Sulfuric acid is used to make fertilizers and to remove rust from iron metal parts. It is also used in car batteries.

## Sulfur in space

Sulfur is often found near volcanoes. Gases from volcanoes contain hydrogen sulfide and sulfur dioxide. These gases react to form the element sulfur.

One of Jupiter's moons, Io, has active volcanoes. It appears yellow in places because of sulfur deposits from its volcanoes.

## Fast Facts

- The old English name for sulfur was brimstone. It means "a stone that burns."
- Burning fuels that contain sulfur produces sulfur dioxide. This is one cause of acid rain.

toxic   poisonous
**wood pulp**   chipped wood with chemicals added, used to make paper

# Halogens

## Saving teeth

In some communities, small amounts of sodium fluoride are added to drinking water. This compound helps prevent tooth **decay** by making teeth stronger. Fluorides are also added to many toothpastes.

Brushing with fluoride toothpaste helps keep teeth healthy.

The halogens are the **elements** found in Group 17 of the **periodic table.** They are all nonmetals with very similar properties. They have many uses in industry.

## Fluorine

Fluorine is a pale yellow, **diatomic** gas. Two of its **atoms** are joined together. But it is much too active to be found in nature as a pure element. Because it is active, it reacts with other elements to form **compounds** called fluorides. Most fluorine is found in **minerals** in the earth's **crust.** These minerals include fluorite and cryolite. Small amounts of fluorine are also found in seawater, teeth, bones, and blood.

Fluorine gas is used in preparing the uranium that is used in the nuclear reactors of power plants. Another use of fluorine is in making the nonstick surfaces of frying pans. The same fluoride is also used in making artificial valves for the heart.

Because chlorine in a water solution kills bacteria, it is used to treat swimming pools. →

**Word Bank**    mineral    nonliving solid material from the earth

# Chlorine

Chlorine is a **poisonous**, yellowish-green diatomic gas. Its name comes from the Greek word *chloros*, meaning "greenish-yellow." In nature, chlorine mostly occurs in **dissolved** salts in seawater and in the deposits in salt mines.

The smell near swimming pools is the **odor** of chlorine. Chlorine compounds are used to kill **bacteria** in the pool water. For the same reason, it is used to treat city water supplies and sewage. Household bleaches used to wash clothes often contain chlorine compounds. Industries also use chlorine bleaches to whiten flour and paper. Another important use of chlorine is in making PVC plastic. This plastic is used to make many products including floor coverings, bicycle seats, garden hoses, and pipes.

## Gas attacks

Chlorine was used in Europe during World War I as a poison gas. Soldiers protected themselves from the gas by soaking cloth in urine and tying it around their noses and mouths. The ammonia in urine reacted with the chlorine and made it safe.

Three months after the first chlorine gas attack, World War I soldiers were given gas masks.

## Preventing fires

Some compounds of bromine help prevent fires and slow the spread of fires. These compounds, called BFRs, are used in the plastic housings for television sets and computer monitors. They are also used in fabric coverings for furniture and mattresses.

## Iodine

Iodine is a shiny, greyish-violet solid at room temperature. It changes directly to a violet gas when heated. Iodine is **poisonous.** It is found in seaweed, in deep wells with salty water, and in some **minerals.** Iodine **compounds** are called iodides.

Because iodine kills **bacteria,** campers often treat water with iodine tablets to make it safe to drink.

Bromine has a wide range of uses, including dyes, medicines, pesticides, and photography.

pesticide    chemical used to kill harmful insects or animals
radioactive    giving off particles or rays and changing to a different element

Iodine is needed to make the **thyroid** gland work properly. Small amounts of sodium iodide are sometimes added to table salt to make sure that people get enough iodine. Sodium iodide is also added to animal feeds in some places. Iodine mixed in alcohol is sometimes used to kill germs on cuts and scrapes. Silver iodide is used in making film for cameras. It can also be added to clouds to make them produce rain faster. This is expensive, but it might help to prevent droughts.

## Bromine

Bromine is a reddish liquid that produces thick, reddish-brown fumes when exposed to air. Bromine is one of only two **elements** that are liquid at room temperature. The other one is the metal mercury. Bromine has a sharp, stinging **odor.** It is very poisonous and can burn the skin. Breathing its fumes can damage the linings of the nose and throat.

Bromine was discovered as a new element in 1826 by a French student. Its name comes from the Greek word bromos, meaning "bad smell." Bromine is found in seawater, in underground salt mines, and in deep wells of salty water. Its compounds are called bromides. Their main uses are in making black-and-white film and in **pesticides.**

### Astatine
Astatine is a very rare element and almost impossible to find in nature. Very little is known about it except that it is **radioactive.** Its name comes from the Greek word astatos, which means "unstable."

RADIATION

This symbol is used to warn that radioactive materials are present.

### Fast Fact
Some newer cars have halogen headlights. The bulbs in these lights contain small amounts of bromine or iodine, which makes the lights very bright.

**thyroid**   gland in the neck that affects children's growth and determines how the body uses food for energy

# Noble Gases

### Breathing heliox

Divers working at high pressures underwater often breathe a **mixture** of helium and oxygen to avoid getting the bends. The helium replaces nitrogen in air, which would **dissolve** into the blood at high pressure. Breathing the heliox mixture makes divers' voices sound strange. Helium makes the divers' vocal cords vibrate faster. So their voices are higher in pitch.

The noble gases are on the far right side of the **periodic table.** All the gases in this group are colorless and **odorless.** They are called noble gases because they do not combine with other **elements** very often.

## Helium

There is a lot of helium in the universe, but there's not very much on the earth. In fact, helium was discovered on the Sun before it was discovered on the earth. Its name comes from the Greek word *helios*, which means "sun." On the earth, most helium is found in natural gas.

Helium is less dense than air. That means it has a smaller **mass** than an equal **volume** of air does. So it is useful for all kinds of balloons, from party balloons to blimps. Scientists also use balloons filled with helium to study and measure conditions high in the **atmosphere.**

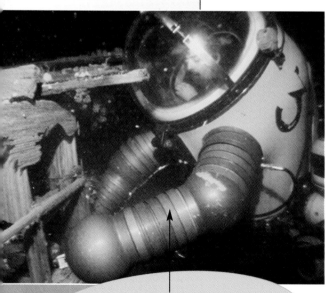

Deep sea divers breathe a mixture of 80 percent helium and 20 percent oxygen.

**Word Bank**   odorless   without smell

## Neon

Neon is the fifth most common gas in the air. It forms no known **compound** with any other element. Neon is used with helium in laser scanners. These kinds of scanners are used at the checkouts in supermarkets. They read the bar codes on food labels and enter the prices. Neon is also used in advertising signs. When electricity is passed through a tube filled with neon gas, the gas gives off an orange-red light.

## Argon

Argon is the third most common gas in the air. It makes up almost one percent of the air. Light bulbs are filled with argon instead of air. In advertising signs, argon gives off a purple light. Only one compound of argon is known. It is a compound of hydrogen, argon, and fluorine.

## A bright idea

Argon inside light bulbs will not react with the metal filament in the light bulb like oxygen in air would. This makes the filament, and the bulb, last longer. It also keeps the inside of the light bulb from turning dark.

Light bulbs do not glow purple because the argon in them is not hot enough.

What people call neon signs usually contain more than one noble gas. Each noble gas produces a different color. "Neon lights" may also have coatings on the inside of the glass tube to give different colored light.

## A few compounds

In 1962 Neil Bartlett of the University of British Columbia made the first compound of a noble gas. The yellow-orange solid is a compound of xenon, platinum, and fluorine. Since then tiny amounts of compounds of krypton, radon, and argon have also been made.

In the 1960s scientists at the Argonne National Laboratory near Chicago created several compounds of xenon.

## Krypton

The earth's **atmosphere** contains one part krypton gas in every 900,000 parts of air. Krypton is used along with argon in some **fluorescent lamps,** and in some flash lamps for high-speed photography. Krypton lights are also used to light landing strips at airports. When electricity is passed through a glass tube containing krypton, a bluish-violet light is given off. Using krypton in lights makes them brighter.

Until the 1960s no **compounds** of krypton were known. Then krypton was found to react with fluorine to form a compound. But only a few grams of it have been made. Tiny amounts of a few other krypton compounds have also been made.

**Word Bank**     fluorescent lamp    electric lamp made out of a tube coated with a powder that glows when electricity is passed through

## Xenon

Xenon only exists in the air in very tiny amounts. But the gas can be separated from the air. Like the other noble gases, it is used in lighting displays. It gives off a bright, white light. It is also sometimes mixed with krypton and used in photographic flash bulbs.

## Radon

Radon is a **radioactive** gas. If it is inhaled it can damage a person's lungs. Radon sometimes seeps into homes from the ground. People living in these homes can get lung cancer if the radon builds up to dangerous levels. Because it damages cells, radon has also been used to treat cancer. It is first pumped into tiny glass vials, called "seeds." The seeds are placed in a person's cancer **tumor. Radiation** from the radon kills the cancer cells but is kept away from normal body cells.

As uranium **decays,** radon gas is produced. This radon monitor is used in homes built on rocks that contain uranium.

Xenon is used in **strobe lights** where short flashes of light are needed for high-speed photography such as sports or action shots.

radiation    rays and particles given off by a radioactive element
tumor    growth of body cells that is not normal and causes a swelling

# Further Information

## Organizations

### Science Made Simple

Learn about science "hands on." Site includes science news, projects, facts, more.
sciencemadesimple.com

### Rader Studios

Fun science news, plus activities including quizzes, experiments, tutorials, and more.
chem4kids.com

### Lawrence Livermore National Laboratory

Get science news from a national security laboratory.
llnl.gov

## Books

Saunders, Nigel. *Neon and the Noble Gases.* Chicago: Heinemann, 2004.

Snedden, Robert. *Material World: Materials Technology.* Chicago: Heinemann, 2001.

Tocci, Salvatore. *The Periodic Table.* Danbury, Conn.: Scholastic, 2003.

## World Wide Web

If you want to find out more about **nonmetals,** you can search the Internet using keywords like these:

- nonmetals + discovery
- "Henry Cavendish"
- carbon + uses
- radon + U.S.
- Daniel Rutherford
- [name of a nonmetal] + properties
- elements + "periodic table"

You can also find your own keywords by using headings or words from this book. Use the search tips opposite to help you find the most useful websites.

## Search tips

There are billions of pages on the Internet so it can be difficult to find exactly what you are looking for. For example, if you just type in "water" on a search engine like Google, you'll get a list of 85 million web pages. These search skills will help you find useful websites more quickly:

- Know exactly what you want to find out about first.
- Use simple keywords instead of whole sentences.
- Use two to six keywords in a search, putting the most important words first.
- Be precise—only use names of people, places, or things.
- If you want to find words that go together, put quote marks around them, for example, "periodic table" or "transition metals."
- Use the advanced section of your search engine.
- Use the + sign to add certain words to your search.

## Where to search

### Search engine

A search engine looks through the entire web and lists all the sites that match the words in the search box. It can give thousands of links, but the best matches are at the top of the list, on the first page. Try **google.com**

### Search directory

A search directory is more like a library of websites that have been sorted by a person instead of a computer. You can search by keyword or subject and browse through the different sites like you would look through books on a library shelf. A good example is **yahooligans.com**

# Glossary

**atmosphere** layer of gases that surround the earth

**atom** smallest particle of an element

**bacteria** tiny living things too small to be seen except with a microscope

**boiling point** temperature at which a liquid changes to a gas

**brittle** firm, but easily broken

**carbohydrate** organic compound that contains carbon, hydrogen, and oxygen

**carbon dating** method of finding out how long ago a plant or animal died by measuring the amount of radioactive carbon left in it

**carbon monoxide** poisonous gas produced as carbon burns when there is not enough oxygen

**chemical reaction** change that produces one or more new substances

**cholesterol** fatty substance in some foods that can clog blood vessels

**coke** form of carbon made from coal

**composition** amount of different materials that make up a substance

**compound** substance made of different kinds of elements joined together

**compressed** squeezed into a smaller space

**conductor** material that heat or electricity can pass through easily

**crust** outer layer of the earth

**decay** rot

**density** mass of a certain volume of something. It is measured in grams per cubic centimeter or kilograms per cubic meter

**diatomic** having atoms of an element joined in pairs

**dissolve** to mix completely and evenly

**dry ice** frozen carbon dioxide

**ductile** able to be stretched into wire

**electron** tiny, negatively charged particle outside the nucleus of an atom

**element** substance made of only one kind of atom

**fertilizer** chemicals added to soil to help plants grow better

**flammable** easily set on fire

**fluorescent lamp** electric lamp made of a tube coated inside with a powder that glows

**fossil** hardened remains of an ancient plant or animal

**fossil fuel** fuel found in the earth's rocks. It was formed from ancient plant and animal life

**fuel** any material that can be burned to produce useful heat or power

**geyser** vent that shoots hot water and steam from underground

**graphite** form of carbon. It is used in pencils, lubricants, and other products.

**greenhouse effect** warming of the earth's climate caused by an increase in carbon dioxide in the air

**insulator** material that heat or electricity cannot pass through easily

**ion** atom or group of atoms that has an electric charge

**lipid** organic compound that includes fats or oils

**lubricant** slippery substance used to make machine parts move smoothly and easily

**luster** shine that metals have

**malleable** able to be hammered, rolled, or shaped without breaking

**mass** amount of matter that makes something up. It is measured in grams or kilograms.

**metalloids** elements that have properties of both metals and nonmetals

**mineral** nonliving solid material from the earth

**mixture** two or more substances that are placed together but not joined

**neutron** uncharged particle in the nucleus of an atom

**nitrogen cycle** circular pathway in which nitrogen moves through the world

**nucleus** dense, positively charged center of an atom

**odor** smell

**odorless** without smell

**opaque** not letting light pass through

**ore** metal that is found combined with other elements

**organic compound** compound that contains carbon

**oxide** compound of oxygen and another element

**ozone** form of oxygen made of three oxygen atoms joined together

**periodic table** chart in which elements are grouped according to similar properties

**pesticide** chemical used to kill harmful insects or animals

**photosynthesis** process by which green plants use sunlight, water, and carbon dioxide to make their own food

**pollutant** harmful substance in the air, water, or land

**pollution** harmful things in the air, water, or land

**protein** organic compound that contains nitrogen and is made up of amino acids

**proton** positively charged particle in the nucleus of an atom

**radiation** rays and particles given off by a radioactive element

**radioactive** giving off particles or rays and changing to a different element

**respiration** process in which a living thing takes in oxygen and uses it to produce energy, giving off carbon dioxide

**smog** haze formed by smoke and other pollutants

**strobe light** very bright light that can flash thousands of times each second

**synthetic** human-made; not natural

**thyroid** gland in the neck that affects children's growth and determines how the body uses food for energy

**translucent** stopping some, but not all, light from passing through

**transparent** letting light pass through

**triatomic** having three atoms of the same element joined together

**tumor** growth of body cells that is not normal and causes a swelling

**volume** amount of space something takes up

**wood pulp** chipped wood with chemicals added. It is used to make paper.

**zeppelin** blimp-like airship

# Index